Power-Packed Spiritual
Copyright © 2019

ISBN 978-1-0884-8216-2 (print)
ISBN 978-0-463-80693-7 (eBook)

TABLE OF CONTENTS

DIVINE GUARANTEES

Ask, and it shall be given you; seek, and you shall find; knock, and it shall be opened unto you: For everyone who asks receives, and whoever seeks finds; and to those who knock it shall be opened. **(Matthew 7:7-8)**

Give, and it will be given to you; a good measure, pressed down, shaken together, and running over, will be poured into you abundantly. For with the same measure that you use for others, it will be measured back to you. **(Luke 6:38)**

Your gift shall make room for you and bring you before great men.
(Proverbs 18:16)

A good name is rather to be chosen than great riches, and loving favor than silver and gold. **(Proverbs 22:1)**

You shall remember the Lord your God for it is He who gives you the power to get wealth. **(Deuteronomy 8:18)**

No good thing will He withhold from those who walk uprightly. **(Psalm 84:11)**

Two are better than one because they have a good reward for their labor.
(Ecclesiastes 4:9)

Wait on the Lord: be of good courage, and He shall strengthen your heart: wait, I say on the Lord. **(Psalm 27:14)**

If My people who are called by My name will humble themselves, and pray and seek My face, and turn from their wicked ways, then I will hear from heaven, and will forgive their sin and heal their land. **(2 Chronicles 7:14)**

If you are faithful in that which is least you will also be faithful with much.
(Luke 16:10)

Beloved, I pray that you may prosper in all things and be in health,
just as your soul prospers.
(3 John 2)

This Book of the Law shall not depart from your mouth, but you shall meditate in it day and night, that you may observe to do according to all that is written in it. For then you will make your way prosperous, and then you will have good success.
(Joshua 1:8)

7 PRAYER DECLARATIONS

1. Thank You God for the gift of life and for blessing me to see a new day.

2. Thank You, Lord, for my family and our beautiful home.

3. Bless my mind and body today and give me energy and wisdom to perform to the best of my abilities.

4. Grant me divine favor and extend my boundaries that I may be a channel of blessing and inspiration to humanity.

5. Bless my extended family and all my friends. Give them peace and guidance today in all their affairs.

6. Bless my team, my associates, my customers and my clients. Bless their families, their health, and their finances. May they find value in the solutions I provide and be able to afford all my products, programs, and services.

7. Protect me as I leave my house today and use me to accomplish Your divine purposes. Amen.

MENTAL DECLARATIONS

1. I am transformed by the renewing of my mind. Therefore, I meditate on the Word of God and apply it to my daily life so that I can make my way prosperous and have good success.

2. As a man thinks in his heart, so is he. Therefore, I think, read, and watch only those things that are true, honorable, just, holy, beautiful, valuable, positive, optimistic, virtuous, and praiseworthy.

3. Wisdom is the principal thing. Therefore, I seek for divine wisdom, knowledge, and understanding in all that I do.

4. I fill my mind with the promises of God for me in every area of my life. Therefore, I claim His blessings of peace, prosperity, pardon, purpose, protection, provision, and promotion today.

5. I believe in lifelong learning. Therefore, I read at least one book a month and always listen to inspirational messages while I drive.

6. I understand the power of the tongue and the influence of my words on my mind, body, and upon others. Therefore, I will only speak positive words of faith, hope, love, courage, exhortation, optimism, enthusiasm, and victory today.

7. God is the source of my success and if He's going to bless me, no one can stop it! Therefore, I express gratitude and joy for all the abundance that will flow my way today.

EMOTIONAL DECLARATIONS

1. I am emotionally and mentally stable. I have peace because my mind constantly dwells upon the Word of God.

2. I do not live in fear, regret, shame, or guilt. In fact, I live by faith, hope, and love. I dwell on the bright side of life and count my many blessings because God is always good to me.

3. I have covenanted to walk by faith and not by sight and feelings. Feelings or no feelings, emotions or no emotions, I do what is right from a sense of principle, love, and duty.

4. My emotions are healthy as they are governed by divine reason. Therefore, I make sound decisions because I lead my heart, feelings, and emotions and not the other way around.

5. The condition of my mind and body affects me emotionally. Therefore, I always keep my mind and body in a healthy state by remaining enthusiastic and positive about life and living. I do not worry about anything, but in everything by prayer and supplication with thanksgiving, I cast all my cares and burdens before God.

6. I do not presume to know everything. Nor am I so arrogant that I cannot be corrected. In fact, today I ask God to grant me a clean heart and pure mind to be a blessing in whatever I do.

7. I freely forgive and hold no grudges. Just as God forgives me, I forgive others – even if they do not ask. I have no need to hold on to guilt or cause others to carry it around. I will make restitution and ask for forgiveness when I do wrong or injure others.

PHYSICAL DECLARATIONS

1. My body is the holy temple of God. Therefore, I will bring my body under divine control and be temperate in all that I eat, drink, and whatsoever I do.

2. I consume high energy nutritious foods consisting of fruits, grains, nuts, and vegetables. I eat a large breakfast, medium lunch, and light supper 5-6 hours apart at the same time daily. I drink at least 8 glasses of water and do not snack between meals.

3. I exercise at least 5 times weekly, preferably outdoors, for 30 minutes to 1 hour. I do both aerobic and anaerobic exercises. I stretch, walk, run, weight train, and play soccer or tennis as part of my daily regimen.

4. I get adequate sunshine daily – at least 15-30 minutes in the open air. I practice deep breathing for 7 repetitions 3 times a day. I inhale a deep breath, hold it for 10-20 seconds, and then release it.

5. I take time for daily, weekly, monthly, and yearly recreation. I go to sleep between 9-10 p.m. and wake up between 5-6 a.m. I enjoy the weekly Sabbath in rest, fellowship, and worship. I take off 1 weekend a month and 2 weeks a year. Every 7 years, I go on a sabbatical to reflect, reassess, and gain new direction.

6. I form good habits and character by the condition of my mind. Therefore, I carefully guard the avenues to my soul by watching what goes into my mind. I choose to think, read, and watch only those things that are wholesome and in keeping with the person I want to become.

7. I speak life and hope into every situation and to everyone I meet. I neutralize all negativity, doubt, and discouragement with my faith and the word of God.

SPIRITUAL DECLARATIONS

1. I love my God with all my heart, soul, mind, and strength. I put Him first and reverence His holy name.

2. I am honest in all that I do and I honor my father, mother, and spouse. I preserve and respect life.

3. I live by every Word that proceeds from the mouth of God. Therefore, I will study, pray, and meditate upon them every day. I will not only read or listen to them but more importantly, I live them – I apply them, I practice them – I do what they say!

4. I take God at His Words by claiming His promises, meeting their conditions, and believing and expecting them to be fulfilled in His time and in His way.

5. I live a radical life of prayer, faith, love, and action. Therefore, I do not worry about failure or defeat because I am more than a conqueror – I can do all things through Christ Who strengthens me.

6. I trust in the Lord with all my heart and lean not to my own understanding but in all my ways, I acknowledge God and He always directs my path. I commit my life into His hand and believe that He will bring my desires to pass.

7. I have no need to fear anyone because no weapon that is formed against me shall prosper and every tongue that rises up against me shall be condemned because this is my heritage as a servant of the Lord who vindicates me.

SOCIAL DECLARATIONS

1.   My greatest relationship after God is my relationship with my spouse and children. Therefore, I do not put work, things, and others before my family and I do not treat others better than I treat them.

2.   I have friends because I am a friend. I value their contributions to my life and I add value to theirs.

3.   I find joy serving humanity with my gifts and talents. I don't just look out for my own goals and happiness but I also help others find their purpose and live out their full potentials.

4.   I have healthy relationships because I practice the Golden Rule Principle. Therefore, I am kind, respectful, and loving. I do for other others the same good things I want them to do for me.

5.   I have 3 very close friends with whom I can be accountable and share personal things in confidence. I have 12 friends in my sphere of influence with whom I can network to achieve success in all areas of my life and with whom I can spend time – enjoying the simpler things of life. I am a faithful contributing member of a local Church and I'm radically involved in impacting the Kingdom with my time, talents, prayers, and financial resources.

6.   I express gratitude today for my family, faith, and finances. I thank You God for Your blessings of health, quality relationships, wisdom, mercies, grace, and love.

7.   I always speak the truth of and to others and as much as possible, I live in peace with everyone. I will compliment my spouse and children for something positive today as well as encourage my associates and anyone I meet.

PROFESSIONAL DECLARATIONS

1. I carry myself in a professional manner. Therefore, I have and set SMART goals – Specific, Measurable, Attainable, Realistic, and Timely. I review my written goals daily and always work from a to-do list.

2. I am diligent in my work. Therefore, whatever I put my hands to I do it with all my might and focus. I start and finish projects on time. I break my goals down into small pieces, and prioritize tasks in order of importance.

3. I am an efficient time manager because time is my greatest entrustment. Therefore, I don't waste time on unimportant distracting things. When I work, I work. When it's time to play, I play hard. When it's time to eat, I do it heartily. When it's time to rest, I do it peacefully.

4. I do what I love and I love what I do. Therefore, I bring passion and compassion into my work. I present my BEST on behalf of humanity. I also exude enthusiasm in all that I do and seek to inspire others to live up to their fullest potentials.

5. I am a solutions provider. Therefore, I seek God for wisdom and direction for answers to all challenges. I keep finding solutions instead of complaints because that's what leaders do – they overcome obstacles and find ways to win.

6. I understand the power and importance of action. Therefore, it's not just what I know, but it's what I do with what I know. To get ahead and to be successful, I must do the good things I know I need to do when I need to do them. No matter what the challenge, I rise to the occasion in God's strength and do what needs to be done. There is never a better time to get things done than right now because once I do them, I'm that much closer to accomplishing my big goal.

7. I am responsible for my life and the outcome. I have a choice and say in how my life actually turns out. Therefore, I have multiple streams of income from books, audio-visual products, online courses, home-based businesses, investments, and divine blessings.

FINANCIAL DECLARATIONS

1. I acknowledge God as the owner of everything! He owns all the wealth and will supply all my needs according to His glorious riches in Christ Jesus. When I Ask, I Receive. When I Seek, I Find. When I Knock, doors Open for me. Praise God for His unspeakable gifts!

2. I am a great steward – a faithful manager of all that God has entrusted in my care. Therefore, I wisely use my time, intellect, mind, body, money, and profession.

3. I am a cheerful giver and believe that God blesses me to be a blessing. Therefore, I cheerfully give 10% from all my increase to building up the kingdom. I also invest another 5-10% as free-will offerings in ministries and causes which God leads me to support.

4. Since I cannot outgive God, I sow bountifully – giving as much as I can and expecting to reap bountifully the blessings of Deuteronomy 28, Psalm 112, and Malachi 3.

5. I live a frugal, modest lifestyle by faithfully managing the remaining monies I have after tithes and offerings. Therefore, I regularly save and invest 10-15% of my income and live on the rest. I have an emergency fund, savings of at least 12 months living expenses, a diversified investment portfolio, a home that's fully paid, and a sizable estate and life insurance policy.

6. I owe no one anything. Therefore, whatever God blesses me above and beyond what is required for my family to live decently, we give and invest it ALL into kingdom enterprises. We send it ahead of us into Heaven's stock market.

7. I do not live in fear of finances because there is no shortage of money and opportunities. There's no need for hoarding because I diversify my giving and stewardship into at least 7 ministries, causes, and projects including: kingdom businesses, evangelism, missionaries, community development, students' debt repayment, the poor, orphans, widows, prisoners, the oppressed, and the sick.

7 KEYS TO WEALTH CREATION

1. I invest in Financial Education through books, courses, seminars, workshops, subscriptions, professional advice, and mentoring.

2. To create generational wealth, Own a few high-quality businesses; Understand those businesses well; Make sure they are in strong, long-term growth industries; Use other people's money prudently; and Hold onto the businesses for the long run and intergenerationally.*

3. I own several Profitable Businesses providing valuable products, programs, and services. I make a great living through publishing, speaking, coaching, consulting, seminars, webinars, eCommerce, affiliate marketing, investing, real estate, and philanthropy.

4. I have Multiple Sources of Residual Income earning me consistent royalties and commissions through books, courses, websites, audio-visual products, joint ventures, rental properties, licenses, and trademarks.

5. I have a Diversified Investment Portfolio that includes charities, private businesses, real estate, stocks, bonds, and mutual funds.

6. Stocks include US large and small caps, Foreign developed equity, Emerging market equity, and Index funds. Mutual funds have a mixture of Growth, Growth and Income, Aggressive Growth, and International funds. Tax Deferred Investments Accounts include Traditional IRA, Roth IRA, SEP IRA, Simple IRA, 401(k), 457(b), 403(b), TSP, HSA, ESA, and 529 plans.

7. I live Debt Free and Drama Free. I own myself and have greater peace of mind and contentment as a result.

* *This investment framework are the 5 Laws of Wealth Creation that all wealthy people implement. It was conceived by billionaire investor, Mr. Michael Lee-Chin.*

7 HIGHLY PRODUCTIVE WORK HABITS

1. I always do my BEST. I am an excellent servant-leader and a dedicated professional. I arrive on time and I leave on time. There's no need for me to bring work home because I will perform above expectations today.

2. I work hard, play hard, eat hard, and rest hard. I'm laser focused and avoid unnecessary interruptions, chit chats, phone calls, and checking emails or social media. To maintain my clear vision, I always ask myself, "What's the most important use of my time, right now?"

3. I acknowledge God as my protector, promoter, and provider. Therefore, I refuse to play office politics or defend myself because my excellent performance speaks for itself.

4. I am Honest in all my business and daily transactions and do not gossip, lie, or cheat in order to get ahead.

5. Because I work for God, I perform as though I am personally accountable to HIM. I am diligent and I glorify God in all I think, say, do, and don't do. I rely on God for wisdom and I trust Him to lead me in the right path.

6. I live the Navy Core Values of Honor, Courage, and Commitment. I am brave enough to make decisions and execute them. I would rather take action than remain indecisive because of fear that I might make mistakes. As the saying goes, "Nothing ventured – nothing gained."

7. Busyness is not a sign of productivity. Therefore, I always work from a "to-do" list. I complete high priority goals and delegate lower priority tasks. I don't multi-task because it increases the time required to finish a task.

7 DAILY SUCCESS HABITS

1. I wake up early (between 5:00 a.m. - 6:00 a.m.). I spend 1 hour or more in prayer, study, meditation, and listening to or watching inspirational messages.

2. I spend 10-15 minutes planning, reviewing, prioritizing, and organizing my day. I will complete 3-7 important tasks on my "to-do" list and delegate low priority tasks to others.

3. I eat a healthy balanced diet consisting of a large breakfast, medium lunch, and a light dinner. I consume high energy foods like fruits, grains, nuts, and vegetables. I drink 7-8 glasses of water daily and do not snack between meals.

4. I do 30 minutes to 1 hour of aerobic and anaerobic exercises. I also stretch, get out doors, garden, play soccer or tennis, and practic deep breathing.

5. I spend 1 hour or more of uninterrupted quality time with my spouse and family. We do fun things together and communicate on an intimate level.

6. I always wind down before going to bed by engaging in personal and professional development. I spend a few moments in quiet reflection on my day – I confess and right all wrongs, get rid of anger, guilt, shame, regrets, worry, and fear.

7. I go to sleep early every night (between 9:00 p.m. - 10:00 p.m.). This gives me a full night's rest because each hour of sleep before midnight is worth two hours of sleep after midnight. I express thanks and gratitude to God for 7-10 things He did for and through me today. Then, I fall asleep in peace.

7 POWERFUL DAILY AFFIRMATIONS

1. Since life and death are in the power of the tongue, I will speak well of situations and people today.

2. Because all things are possible with God, all things are possible for me and I will achieve all my goals and make a difference.

3. I have no need to worry about material possessions because I put God's kingdom first in my life and I'm blessed and highly favored.

4. God has not given me a spirit of fear, but of power, love and a sound mind. Therefore, I shall be the head and not the tail. I will make a lasting impact, fund my dreams, and sustain my mission, message, and cause.

5. I love my Wonderful, Marvelous Spouse. I couldn't ask for a better life partner who loves me and treats me like royalty.

6. My body radiates health and vitality. I will exude positive energy and optimism in all that I do today.

7. What my mind can conceive and believe, with the blessing of God, I can and will achieve. Therefore, I expect to be successful and productive today.

7 AFFIRMATIONS FOR A HEALTHY SELF-IMAGE

1. I am fearfully and wonderfully made. I live a victorious, harmonious, and balanced spiritual life and practice what I believe.

2. I live by sound principles. Since I'm called to love others as I love myself, then the quality of my love for others is a direct reflection of how I love myself.

3. I am a loving and understanding spouse and parent. I affirm and show kindness and compassion to my family by my words and actions.

4. I am an intelligent and valuable person. I add value and impart goodness to every person, ministry, and organization with whom I'm associated.

5. I am healthy and energetic! I take excellent care of my body by eating right and exercising regularly. I speak the way I want to be (not the way I am) because the day will come when I will be the way I speak.

6. I am successful, prosperous, and generous. There is no shortage of resources and opportunities abound everywhere. God blesses me daily so that I can be a blessing to others. I sow bountifully, therefore, I always expect to reap bountifully.

7. I am Honest, Loyal, and Diligent. I treat people with respect and help them realize their full potential. Because I'm blessed and highly favored, I always acknowledge God as my provider, promoter, protector, and peace.

7 KEYS TO SPICE UP ANY MARRIAGE

1. Say "I Love you" 3-7 times a day. Love is the golden word of life.

2. Hug and Kiss 3-7 times a day. It's good for health, healing, and longevity.

3. Enjoy love-making 4-6 times a week. It keeps the bedroom hot.

4. Compliment each other on something positive 3-5 times a day. Words shape behavior, habits, and character so choose them wisely.

5. Spend no less than 1 hour of uninterrupted time together daily and 1 full day each week. Do fun things together and communicate openly.

6. Pray with and for each other and worship together regularly during the week. This practice glues marriages and families together.

7. Make things right with each other before going to sleep. Don't let the sun go down while you're still angry. Be humble and forgive each other.

7 CORE LIFE PRINCIPLES

1. I Love God with all my Heart, Mind, Soul, and Strength.

2. I Love my neighbor as I love myself.

3. I choose to be happy and joyful and will use my unique gifts and talents to bless as many people as possible.

4. I owe no man anything except to love all people as God loves them.

5. I think, read, watch, and do things that are true, noble, just, pure, lovely, of good report, virtuous, positive, optimistic, and praiseworthy.

6. I trust God's words and apply them to all facets of my life.

7. I believe in the power of prayer and action and do both consistently.

7 SUCCESS PRINCIPLES

1. I always think, pray, and act in faith. It's the best way to live.

2. I always speak words of Courage, Hope, and Truth. Anything less is unacceptable.

3. I always do my BEST and leave the results with God. I can only do my part and only God can do His part.

4. I never rely solely on feelings and emotions. I live by faith and sound principles.

5. I never speak words of fear, doubt, or discouragement. I am more than a conqueror through Jesus Christ and I can do all things through His strength.

6. I never utter one word of failure or can't in my work. God cannot fail and because I work for Him, I always succeed.

7. I never take reward or honor for the works of God. He is the true miracle worker.

7 GOLDEN RULE PRINCIPLES

1. I do everything possible on my part to live in peace with everyone.

2. I do for others the same good things I desire them to do for me.

3. I give honor, respect, and credit where it is due.

4. I do good to those who hate me. I bless those who curse me. I pray for those who use and persecute me.

5. I do not avenge myself by trying to repay evil for evil. Instead, I conquer evil with good and leave all judgment and recompense up to God. He is merciful, faithful, just, and loving.

6. If my enemy or competitor is hungry, I'll share my food. If they're thirsty, I'll give a drink. If they're in a ditch or bind, I'll lend a helping hand.

7. I refrain from gossip and condemning people, ministries, and institutions. Instead, I speak well of them and if I have nothing positive to say, I hold my peace.

7 FAVORITE SCRIPTURE VERSES

1. God is not a man, that He should lie, nor a son of man, that He should repent. Has He said, and will He not do it? Or has He spoken, and will He not make it good? In hope of eternal life which God, Who cannot lie, promised before the world began. (Numbers 23:19; Titus 1:2)

2. This is the declaration of the Lord GOD, "None of My words will be delayed any more, but the word which I speak will be done," says the Lord GOD. "So shall My word be that goes forth out of My mouth; it shall not return to Me empty, but it shall accomplish that which I please, and it shall prosper in the thing for which I sent it." (Ezekiel 12:28; Isaiah 55:11)

3. Whoever wins souls is wise. Those who are wise will shine like the brightness of the expanse of heaven; and they who turn many to righteousness as the stars for ever and ever. (Proverbs 11:30; Daniel 12:3)

4. I trust in the Lord, and do good; so will I dwell in the land, and verily I shall be well fed. I delight myself also in the Lord, and He will give me the desires of my heart. I commit my way unto the Lord, trust also in Him, and He shall bring it to pass. He will bring forth my righteousness as the light, and my justice as the noonday. I rest in the Lord, and wait patiently for Him. I do not fret myself because of those who prosper in their way, because of the one who carries out wicked schemes. (Psalm 37:3-7)

5. I am not so conceited to assume that I know it all. Instead, I trust and respect the Lord, and stay away from evil. When I do this, it brings health to my body and strength to my bones. (Proverbs 3:7, 8)

6. The peace of God, which surpasses all understanding, will guard my heart and mind in Christ Jesus. (Philippians 4:7)

7. Now unto Him Who is able to do exceeding abundantly above all that I ask or think, according to the power that works in me. As it is written, eye has not seen, nor ear heard, nor have entered into the heart of mankind, the (good) things which God has prepared for me because I love Him. (Ephesians 3:20; 1 Corinthians 2:9)

7 DYNAMIC BREAKTHROUGH PROMISES

1. Whatever things I ask for when I pray, I believe that I receive them, and therefore, I will have them. If two of us (or more) agree together on earth concerning anything that we pray about, which is in harmony with the will of God, it shall be done for us by my Father in heaven. (Mark 11:24; Matthew 18:19)

2. When I bring the full amount of all my tithes into God's Treasury, so that there will be plenty of resources in His Temple, the Lord Almighty says, "Prove Me in this, and see if I will not open the windows of heaven for you, and pour out so many blessings on you, that you will not have enough room to receive them all." (Malachi 3:10)

3. If I confess my sins, God is faithful and just to forgive me of my all sins, and to cleanse me from all unrighteousness. Whoever conceals their sins will not prosper, but whoever confesses and forsakes them will have mercy. (1 John 1:9; Proverbs 28:13)

4. Bless the LORD, O my soul, and forget not all His benefits: Who forgives all my iniquities, Who heals all my diseases, Who redeems my life from destruction, Who crowns me with loving-kindness and tender mercies, Who satisfies my mouth with good things, so that my youth is renewed like the eagle's. (Psalm 103:2-5)

5. No temptation has overtaken me except such as is common to mankind; but God is faithful, Who will not allow me to be tempted beyond what I am able, but will with the temptation also make a way to escape, that I may be able to bear it. (1 Corinthians 10:13)

6. God has declared, "And it shall come to pass afterward, that I will pour out My Spirit on all people; and your sons and daughters shall prophesy, your old men shall dream dreams, your young men shall see visions. In those days, I will also pour out My Spirit on My servants, both men and women." (Joel 2:28-29)

7. Because I delight in the law of the LORD, and in His law I meditate day and night, I will be like a tree planted by the rivers of water, that brings forth fruit in its season. Whose leaf also shall not wither; and whatever I do will prosper. (Psalm 1:2-3)

MY DECLARATIONS OF DESIRE

1. I decree and declare that I will make a lasting impact, fund my dreams, and sustain my mission, message, and cause.

2. I decree and declare that I will live up to my full potentials, achieve greatness, and enjoy time, money, location, and relationship freedom.

3. I decree and declare that I will live _____ _____ and drive my dream _____.

4. I decree and declare that I will easily and consistently make $ _____ a week, $ _____ a month and $ _____ a year.

5. I decree and declare that I will give $_____, save $ _____, and invest $ _____ a month/year.

6. I decree and declare that I will see and travel to _____ _____ by _____ _____ (date).

7. I decree and declare that my legacy and major contribution in life will be _____ _____ _____ _____ _____.

CREATE YOUR OWN AFFIRMATIONS

CPSIA information can be obtained
at www.ICGtesting.com
Printed in the USA
BVHW011249100620
581263BV00004B/95

9 781088 482162